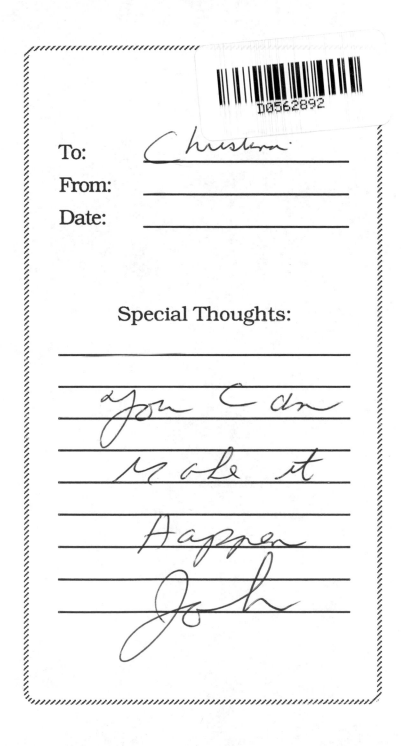

To: Christina

From:

Date:

Special Thoughts:

You Can
Make it
Happen
John

THE
BIG
SECRET

by
John J. Pelizza, Ph.D.

Published by:
Pelizza & Associates
P.O. Box 225
North Chatham, New York 12132

Edited by: Phillip Niles

Cover & Text Design by: Bonnie S. Pelizza

Illustrations by: Kimberly P. Hart

Poem by: Joe McGee

Advisory Panel:

Teri Bopp, First Grade Teacher, Ichabod Crane Central School District, Valatie, New York

Linda Jackson-Chalmers, Principal, Arbor Hill Elementary School, Albany, New York

Lois Etkin, Remedial Reading Teacher, Mont Pleasant Middle School, Schenectady, New York

Joseph Prenoveau, Ed.D., Assistant Superintendent for Instruction, South Colonie School District, Albany, New York

Elaine Kern, Elementary Teacher, Erie, Pennsylvania

Published by Pelizza & Associates, P.O. Box 225, North Chatham, New York 12132, (518) 766-4849.

Printed and bound in the United States of America.
ISBN 0-9614782-3-2

DEDICATION

This book is dedicated to my loving wife, Bonnie, and two sons, Tony and Joe, who encouraged me to write and share . . . .
. . . . "The Big Secret."

FOREWORD

The story of Jamie typifies the growth process that all children must experience in order to develop a healthy attitude towards success and failure. In today's society our children are continually bombarded with a myriad of positive and negative images, situations, issues and choices, frequently without the benefit of a clear moral code or direction on which to base their opinions or to make appropriate decisions.

The Big Secret is a charming tale which will help kids visualize that mistakes, disappointments and, yes, failures are not fatal. The story reveals that learning through life's ups and downs strengthens individual character and builds personal endurance for a successful life.

Our school, serving a very challenged urban community, has been involved in school improvement issues for many years.

We strongly believe in addressing the needs of the "whole" child and teaching that child coping skills to better handle stress, disappointment and frustration.

We have had the wonderful opportunity to work with Dr. Pelizza. His wellness presentation has inspired and exhilarated the faculty and staff of the Arbor Hill School as we continue to refine our child centered community school program. He has taught us to live with our successes and failures, to feel better. . . good.

It is only natural that Dr. Pelizza's unique talent should now address the well being of children as he has so successfully done with adults.

Through Jamie's tale many youngsters will learn a valuable lesson of life and discover a <u>Big Secret.</u>

Linda Jackson-Chalmers
Principal
Arbor Hill Elementary
       Community School
Albany, New York

"The Big Secret - This short story explores the important life lesson of learning to fail in order to succeed. A lesson that no child nor adult escapes from, but could learn and grow from. Written in an easy to comprehend, short story format, The Big Secret could be used by teachers as a tool to incorporate self-esteem lessons into their reading programs - at any level."

Teri Bopp
First Grade Teacher

"I teach remedial reading to sixth grade students at Mont Pleasant Middle School. Many of the students I teach are having a difficult time at school. Your book was perfect for my students. Not only did they enjoy the story, they also received the message. Reading your book allowed my students to feel better about themselves. Thank you for the opportunity to share your book with my students."

Lois Etkin
Remedial Reading Teacher

"Parents will be thrilled to share and read <u>The Big Secret</u> with their children!"

Joseph Prenoveau, Ed.D.
Assistant Superintendent
for Instruction

"I really feel you were able to get inside a 5th grader's head and convey what they must be feeling a lot of the time. They are at the point in their lives where on one hand they seek independence from their parents and want to start making their own decisions, yet on the other hand they lack the self-confidence and conviction to do this without feeling just the way Jamie did in the story. I really feel you've achieved your objective of teaching them to be more tolerant of their own failures in an imaginative and creative way that will hold their interest."

Elaine Kern
Parent and Elementary Teacher

The
Big Secret

Once there was a young person named Jamie.

Jamie was a pretty normal kid. In fact, you might know somebody just like Jamie.

Jamie lived in a nice house in a good neighborhood. Jamie had parents who loved Jamie and treated Jamie well. Jamie had a dog named Bosco, a cat named Spunkie -- and even a hamster named Sunny which Jamie's parents had given Jamie a couple of birthdays ago.

All in all, Jamie had a very good life.

But...

Something was bothering Jamie lately.

Jamie was a good student, and had always done very well in school. Jamie's teachers praised Jamie, and Mom and Dad would smile every time Jamie brought home a report card. "Oh, Jamie," they would beam, "you make us so proud!"

But something had changed. This year in school was different. The subjects seemed harder. For the first time ever, Jamie's parents saw a "C" on Jamie's report card. They still beamed and said they were proud, but somehow it wasn't the same. Was there something Jamie didn't understand? Some secret, perhaps?

"You know," Jamie said one day to Bosco, just thinking out loud, "school used to be easy, old buddy, but this year s u r e is different!"

**And
then
it
happened!**

Miss Mellon, Jamie's math teacher, came into math class on Monday and passed back her weekly test, just like she always did. But this time, at the top of the paper Jamie saw something Jamie had never seen before. Not ever -- not in Jamie's whole life. A big red "F," with the words, "What's wrong, Jamie? You need to do much, much better."

A
big
red "F"

Maybe it was a really
hard test, Jamie thought.
Jamie looked across the row
at Chris, Jamie's friend.
Chris held up a paper with a
big "A" at the top, with the
words, "Great job! Keep up the
good work, Chris!!"

Jamie's heart sank. Then it started to pound. And pound. And pound. Jamie felt a kind of pain that Jamie had never felt before.

What would Jamie's parents say?

Even though Mom and Dad had taught Jamie always to be honest, this time Jamie decided things were different. Jamie decided not to tell them about the "big red F." After all, Jamie was doing OK in math, and Jamie knew it was possible to raise your grade by the end of the marking period. At least, that's what Jamie thought.

It wasn't like Jamie's parents expected Jamie to be perfect or anything like that. Jamie knew they'd both had plenty of problems themselves. Both Mom and Dad had been married before, and Jamie even had a brother, Jimmy, from Dad's first marriage, although Jamie didn't see Jimmy very often since he lived with Dad's former wife.

Jamie sometimes heard Mom and Dad call their first marriages "mistakes," so Jamie knew it wasn't the end of the world if you messed up.

Jamie's dad had even

lost his job a few years ago, but, after being out of work for a while, he still managed to get a better one. What Jamie didn't understand was why this new problem bothered Jamie so much -- why the pain hurt Jamie so bad.

On the way home Jamie asked, "What happened?" Jamie <u>was</u> playing ball this year. That much was different. But Jamie still had enough time for homework. And Jamie was trying as hard as ever. Some kids in Jamie's class never seemed to try. They goofed off and didn't study. It almost seemed they CHOSE to fail, somehow.

But Jamie really <u>wanted</u> to do well.

What went wrong? What was the "big secret"?

What was the "big secret?"

MY IDEAS:

On the lines below, write down what you think is the "big secret."

_____

_____

_____

_____

_____

_____

_____

_____

_____

_____

_____

_____

After getting home, Jamie had a snack, grabbed a mitt, and headed for practice. Fielding ground balls, shagging flies, and hitting line drives made Jamie forget all about math class and Miss Mellon -- almost. It was when Jamie watched Chris, who was also on Jamie's team, hit a home run that Jamie remembered the "big red F," and Jamie felt the pain again.

The
big
red "F"

MY IDEAS:

On the lines below, write down the times you have felt like Jamie.

_____

_____

_____

_____

_____

_____

_____

_____

_____

_____

_____

_____

_____

That night after dinner Jamie got right to work. Jamie took out a book and started on math homework right away. After a while the phone rang, but Jamie was working so hard that Jamie barely even heard it.

A few minutes later there was a knock on the door. It was Jamie's dad.

One look at Dad's face and Jamie knew. Miss Mellon had called.

"I'm really sorry, Dad," Jamie said. "I'm trying really hard. I really am. I just don't know what happened."

Dad sat down next to

Jamie and put his arm around Jamie. "That's what Miss Mellon said, too. She explained that you're doing some different math this year, and that you might need some extra help. You don't have practice on Wednesdays or Fridays. Maybe you can see her then."

Jamie looked at Dad and made an effort to smile. "OK, I'll try."

"Trying isn't enough, Jamie. You have to <u>do</u> it."

"OK," Jamie agreed. "I'll do it."

Jamie's father got up to go.

"And Dad?"

"Yes, Jamie?"

"You know that paint set you bought me for Christmas? The one with all those oil paints -- and the easel?"

"Yes, Jamie. Did you ever get to use them?"

"Well, I was looking at the paint set last week, and I'm going to paint a picture, Dad. A portrait of Grandma -- from that old photo I found, remember? And I'm going to finish it in two weeks!"

"That's terrific, Jamie! What a great idea! We'll both love it!"

Jamie's dad left. Jamie was a little puzzled, though. Dad seemed OK about this math thing, but what did he really think?

The next two weeks Jamie worked hard. Harder than Jamie had ever worked in Jamie's whole life! Jamie studied, Jamie saw Miss Mellon twice after school, and Jamie started to paint the portrait of Jamie's grandmother.

When Jamie got the next math test back, Jamie saw a "D" at the top of the paper. Not good -- but BETTER, Jamie thought. But

Jamie still felt a little of the strange pain, though. So Jamie decided to stay after class and ask Miss Mellon about it. Maybe she knew "the secret."

Does she know the secret????

"Hello, Jamie," Miss Mellon said. "You did much better on your test this week."

"I did?" Jamie asked. "But I only got a 'D'!"

Miss Mellon smiled. "Sit down, Jamie."

Jamie took a seat in the front row.

"Now," began Miss Mellon. "Why is a 'D' so bad?"

"Well," answered Jamie, "I mean, it's a . . . . a 'D.' It's barely passing, right? I mean, nobody wants to get a 'D,' Miss Mellon."

"You're right, Jamie," Miss Mellon agreed, "nobody

<u>does</u> want to get a 'D,' and I'm glad <u>you're</u> not happy with one. But," added Miss Mellon as she picked up a piece of chalk, "I'd like to show you something."

Miss Mellon drew a diagram on the board for Jamie.

"Now, Jamie," Miss Mellon explained, "the lowest grade you could have earned on this test is a zero, right?"

Jamie thought about this for a while. "I suppose so, but I'd never get a zero, Miss Mellon. I mean, I do know <u>something</u>!"

I
do
know
something!!!

Miss Mellon laughed. "Of course, Jamie. "And that's the point!" She turned back to the blackboard. "Now, the 'D' you got on your last test was a 72, right?"

"Yes."

Miss Mellon pointed at the line which marked "72" on her diagram. "72 is not close to zero." She traced out the distance between these two numbers with her finger. "A long way, right?"

Jamie seemed to understand what Miss Mellon was getting at, but was still a little confused. Yes, it is a long way from zero. But it's still a 'D'."

"Yes, that's true, Jamie. But what does all that space between zero and 72 tell us about your performance?"

Jamie looked at the diagram, and thought and thought. Jamie still wasn't sure about all this, but decided to give it a try anyway. "That I've learned some of the stuff?"

"Exactly!" said Miss Mellon brightly. "But not just some of the material. A lot of the material! You've learned and grown -- even though your test level is only a 'D.' Can you see that, Jamie?"

Jamie looked at the

diagram, and suddenly Jamie understood. A lot of times when teachers asked you to "see" things, you didn't. Not really. But this time Jamie really <u>did</u> see! Even a 72 -- a "D" -- wasn't as bad as Jamie first thought. Because even a "D" showed Jamie had learned and grown! Wow! Was this "the secret"?

??? ????

MY IDEAS:

On the lines below, write down when you have said you understood something and you really didn't. This could be with a teacher or parent or friend.

_____

_____

_____

_____

_____

_____

_____

_____

_____

Jamie looked up to find Miss Mellon smiling happily. "You <u>do</u> see, don't you, Jamie?"

Jamie nodded in agreement.

"And," Miss Mellon concluded, "there's something else, too. Something even BETTER, Jamie. Something I'm not sure you've realized yet."

"What's that, Miss Mellon?" Jamie asked eagerly.

What's that?

Miss Mellon smiled warmly, yet a little mysteriously. "I think you need to figure that out for yourself, Jamie. Or, perhaps with the help of a close personal friend."

???

Jamie wondered what Miss Mellon meant exactly, but accepted her answer. "OK, Miss Mellon. Thanks a lot. I'll be in for some more help on Wednesday."

"Good for you, Jamie. See you then."

Let's play ball!

On Friday Jamie played in the first game of the season. Jamie's mom and dad were there, along with most of Jamie's friends from school. The first time up, Jamie got a hit. And then another hit a few innings later! Jamie's team was winning, and everything was just great!

But . . .

Late in the game Jamie's team ran into some trouble. Their pitcher walked the bases loaded with two outs. The next batter swung and missed the first time, but hit the second pitch toward left field. Right where Jamie was playing.

"I've got it! I've got it!" Jamie yelled as the ball approached.

But . . .

Something happened.

Jamie hadn't run back far enough!

The ball hit the top of Jamie's mitt and rolled to the fence.

But . . .

All the runners scored, and Jamie's team was behind.

The next batter struck out. Jamie slowly walked into the dugout, head down, and sat in the corner.

Luckily, Jamie's team won anyway. Chris hit a home run in the last inning, and everybody jumped up and down. Jamie jumped up and down, too, but deep down Jamie knew what had happened. It was the "big red F" a second time. Jamie had failed -- again.

Failed again!

Jamie remembered Miss Mellon's words about "learning and growth," but the pain was still there. What <u>was</u> this "secret" Jamie was missing?

??????

The next day at school some of Jamie's friends were looking at Jamie "funny." At least that's what Jamie thought. Maybe they weren't, really, but something sure seemed different. In the hall Jamie even thought somebody said, "Loser," but it might have been just Jamie's imagination. Jamie felt that way a lot lately -- that things were different.

Even Jamie's parents seemed a little odd.   At dinner, they were a little too cheerful -- a little <u>too</u> nice to Jamie.

**Things
sure don't
seem
the same.**

Things
just seem
different!!!

MY IDEAS:

On the lines below, write down when you have felt that people were looking at you funny.

_____

_____

_____

_____

_____

Were they really?

_____

_____

_____

_____

_____

_____

That night Jamie worked harder than ever on the painting of Jamie's grandmother. The old, yellowed photograph Jamie was working from was kind of fuzzy and didn't help much, but Jamie was confident that the portrait would still turn out well. Jamie wanted to prove something to Mom and Dad. Jamie wanted to do things <u>right</u>. "I'll show them I'm not a failure," Jamie said while petting Bosco. "They'll see."

The next day Jamie went up to the attic. Jamie was looking for an old baseball glove from a couple of years ago. One that was bigger than the glove Jamie was using now. A mitt that would help Jamie catch fly balls.

Bosco was with Jamie for a while, but suddenly he disappeared back down the stairs. Jamie's cat Spunkie put in an appearance, looking around at everything curiously, but she didn't stick around long either. Now alone, Jamie pulled down a very old and dusty box and started to rummage through it.

Inside the box was the baseball mitt Jamie was looking for -- and a very strange-looking bottle. In fact, it was so strange-looking that Jamie set down the baseball glove and picked up the bottle instead.

This bottle was sort of green in color and shaped like one Jamie had seen in a museum on a school field trip. It was incredibly dusty -- so dusty that Jamie blew on it. But the dust wouldn't budge. So Jamie started to rub the bottle. Jamie rubbed and rubbed and rubbed. Jamie was starting to see some kind of writing on the outside of the bottle when suddenly. . .

CRASH!!!

There was a sound like thunder, a flash like lightning, and blue smoke began to pour out of the bottle.

As Jamie watched, amazed, the smoke spun round and round. Before long it took shape. The shape of a chubby little man. A chubby little man in a white suit. But instead of a turban on top of his head, the little chubby man wore a baseball cap!

"Hi," said the man. "I'm Joe."

"Joe?"

"That's right. Joe!"

"Are you a genie?" Jamie gasped.

"Well, I prefer 'Spirit from the Bottle,' but if you'd rather say 'genie,' then <u>genie</u> it is!"

"Do I get three wishes?"
Jamie asked.

Three wishes????

"Gee!" exclaimed Joe.
"You sure don't waste time!
And that's good Jamie,
because I don't either!" Joe
laughed out loud. "So you
want to know if you get three
wishes? Well, I'm afraid not."

"No?" Jamie protested.
"But I thought genies <u>always</u>
granted three wishes!"

Joe laughed again, and
his baseball cap bobbed up
and down. "That's only in

stories," Joe explained. "But "three" _is_ the right idea, Jamie. You're on the right track there."

"What do you mean?" Jamie asked, noticing for the first time that he could see right through Joe, all the way to the back wall of the attic.

"Well, I'm going to take you on _three_ short trips, Jamie. Nothing major. Don't worry, you'll be back by dinner time. But first -- as a friend, mind you -- let me ask you something. Jamie, just how have you been feeling lately?"

Jamie's heart sank again, and the pain came back. Jamie felt it was a good idea to level with Joe, though. After all, how could you lie to a genie?

"Pretty rotten," Jamie replied.

"Oh! Why?" Joe inquired, rubbing his nose.

Jamie hesitated. "Well, I......I......"

"Spit it out," Joe urged. "After all, it's only words."

"I . . . FAILED!" Jamie blurted, and then there was silence. "I got an 'F' on a math test, and I dropped a fly ball."

I failed!

I got an "F"
and
I dropped . . . .
a
fly ball.

MY IDEAS:

On the lines below, write down when you have failed.

_____

_____

_____

_____

_____

_____

_____

_____

_____

_____

_____

_____

Strangely, though, Joe laughed. "You think that's bad, Jamie? I've been trying to get out of this bottle for 50 years!"

Joe roared with laughter. But Jamie wasn't amused. Jamie still felt bad.

"Tell you what," suggested Joe, lifting up his baseball cap and scratching his bald head. "I know how you're feeling. I really do. And I want you to see three things that will make you feel BETTER. OK with you?"

"Sure," Jamie agreed, even though Jamie wasn't. "Where are we going?"

"Into your future, Jamie."

Jamie's future????

Joe snapped his fingers on both of his hands and -- suddenly -- the attic was gone.

Jamie and Joe were now standing near the stage of a large auditorium. An auditorium filled with people. Some of the people were wearing blue robes, and one of them was giving a great speech.

"Where are we?" Jamie whispered.

"You don't know?" Joe replied. "This is your high-school graduation, Jamie."

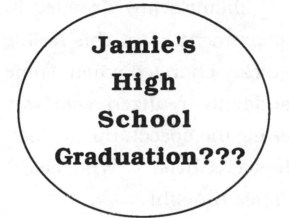

Jamie's
High
School
Graduation???

"What? That's <u>years</u> from now!"

"Exactly!" commented Joe. "Recognize that tall kid sitting on the aisle in the third row?"

Jamie looked. "No. Who is it?"

"Who is it?" Joe laughed. "Why, that's _you_, Jamie!"

Jamie's jaw dropped in amazement. But this feeling quickly changed when Jamie suddenly realized who was giving the speech up on stage. It was Chris. "Who else?" Jamie thought.

Who else????

Chris Jones
Class
President

"We must face the challenge of our futures," Chris was saying. "We must make three words the cornerstone of all our goals -- TO BE SUCCESSFUL. We must not FAIL!"

Everybody applauded. Jamie's parents, sitting in the first row of the audience, clapped enthusiastically -- and beamed, as usual. Jamie was wondering if they'd rather have Chris for their child.

"This was supposed to help me feel BETTER?" Jamie asked Joe as the applause went on and people began to cheer.

Joe laughed once more. "We're just getting started, Jamie!"

We're just getting started.

Now everyone in the auditorium stood up to applaud Chris' stirring words.

"By the way," Joe said over the noise, "have you ever heard of Brooks Robinson?"

"Brooks Robinson!" Jamie shouted. "Of course! He was the greatest third baseman who ever lived. He could..."

"Did you know," interrupted Joe, "that he once made three errors?"

"Wow! Three errors. In one game?"

Joe smiled. "In one inning."

"In one inning!" Jamie exclaimed, but the words were lost as Joe snapped his fingers again and the scene changed.

On

to

trip

two!

This time Joe and Jamie were in a big city, in front of a tall building. Over the entrance to the building appeared the words, "GLOBAL MANAGEMENT CORPORATION."

"Where are we now?"
Jamie asked, looking up,
amazed.

"We're 30 years in the
future!" Joe answered.

"Thirty years!"

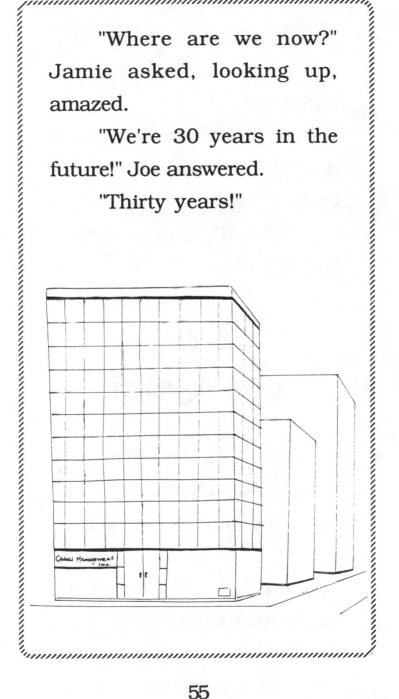

"That's right, Jamie."

"And what's this big building?"

Joe laughed and laughed. "This is where Chris works!"

"Chris!" Jamie cried. "Not again!"

Chris, not again!

"Yes, Chris! Did you know that Chris had the same ambition as you back in school?"

"Really? You mean, to run a business some day?"

"You've got it!" Joe stated. "Want to see how Chris did?"

Jamie sighed. "Do I have a choice?"

Joe roared again. "No. I'm a <u>real</u> genie, remember?"

Suddenly Jamie and Joe were in an office. On the door, in blue letters, were the words, "New Accounts."

"Nobody can see us," Joe whispered in Jamie's ear, "but we'd better stay back in this corner, anyway. Now watch carefully."

Into the office walked a middle-aged person in plain-looking gray clothes. A person who sighed out loud while sitting down at the desk, and moved a few folders without enthusiasm. Who looked very tired. Worst of all, Jamie noticed, a person who looked <u>old</u>.

"Is that <u>Chris</u>?" Jamie asked, with eyes wide.

"Absolutely," answered Joe with his big smile and wink.

"You mean, it's really Chris!"

"That's Chris, Jamie. Your friend. Watch."

A very efficient-looking secretary entered into the office. "Good morning!" she bubbled with a great deal of enthusiasm.

Chris answered automatically, "Good morning, Mrs. Walker."

The secretary cleared her throat. "Miss Rand would like to see you at ten o'clock. She didn't seem too happy about the report we sent over to her yesterday afternoon."

Chris sighed again, and slumped in the chair. "Tell her I'll be right up, Mrs. Walker. Maybe someday I'll get things right."

Now, suddenly, Jamie and Joe were right back in

the street in front of the great big building where Chris worked.

"You mean," Jamie blurted, "that Chris doesn't run this company? Chris isn't the president, or anything like that?"

"Nope," answered Joe. "Not even close."

Jamie was silent for a while. "What happened?"

"Well," explained Joe as they sat down on a bench. "Chris <u>did</u> start a company after leaving college, but it didn't work out that well."

"Really?" Jamie asked. "How is that possible? Chris

succeeded at everything --
school, sports, everything!"

Joe laughed once more,
and scratched his ear.
"Maybe so, but, well, you see,
life's a little different than
school, Jamie."

Life's
different!!

"Is it? My dad says that
all the time. I guess he's
right, then."

Joe smiled. "He sure is,
Jamie. And, you see, Chris
never learned something
which you <u>have</u> to know to
really succeed in life."

"What?" Jamie yelled as a taxi passed by, honking its horn loudly. "Chris always got the best grades in school -- straight A's!"

"Yes, that's true, Jamie," Joe commented, then paused. "But, you see, Chris never learned how to do one very, very important thing."

"What's that?" Jamie inquired. Could this be <u>the big secret?</u>

The
big
secret???

Time seemed to stand still for a moment, until Joe finally spoke. "How to FAIL."

How
to
FAIL!

How could
that be
the secret?

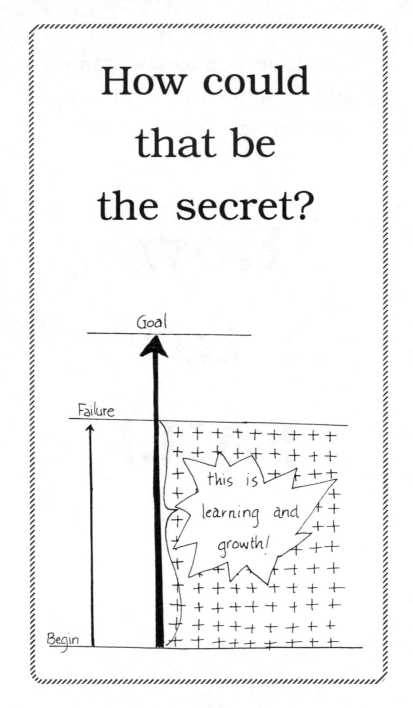

Jamie looked up in amazement. How to FAIL? How could that be the secret? It didn't sound right, somehow. But Jamie decided to hear Joe out, anyway.

Joe made himself more comfortable on the bench. "Did you ever see Chris get an 'F' in school?"

"Never," Jamie admitted.

"Did you ever see Chris drop a fly ball?"

You've got to be kidding!

Jamie chuckled. "You've got to be kidding! Chris was the one who hit home runs to win the game after I dropped the fly ball!"

Joe laughed long and loud. "And that's my point, Jamie. You see," Joe explained, "running your own business is really, really hard. When Chris' company had some problems in the first few years -- as all new businesses do -- Chris couldn't handle it. Chris never really had trouble with anything before, so Chris didn't know what to do when things went wrong. Chris got very upset -- with Chris. Chris saw the problems as a failure. Chris sold the business after a while, and has been working here ever since."

Head on hands, Jamie was obviously deep in thought. "Chris didn't look very happy."

"How <u>could</u> Chris be happy?" Joe remarked. "What Chris wanted most was to run a business, right? After all, isn't the whole idea to do what you <u>really</u> want with your life?"

?????

Jamie knew there was no need to answer this question.

"Before our last stop," Joe finally said, let me ask you a question or two. OK?"

"Sure."

"When you got the 'big red F' in math, what did you do?"

??????

"Well, I went in to see Miss Mellon for extra help, and I studied a lot harder."

"Did you give up?"

"Well, no."

"Did you go on learning -- and growing?"

Learning
and
growing???

"Well, I think so," Jamie said. Hey, Jamie thought, "learning and growing" -- the same words Miss Mellon used. Maybe this really <u>was</u> the secret!

Joe smiled once more. He seemed to read Jamie's thoughts somehow. "And how about the baseball game, Jamie? You dropped a fly ball in front of your whole team and your friends and your family. But . . . are you going to be back out there for the next game?"

"Well, sure," Jamie said, becoming suddenly enthusiastic, "I was even looking for a better glove to help me play better. Hey, that's how I met you!"

"Good for you! You see, Jamie," Joe said in a deep voice. "Sooner or later everybody fails at something important. After all, not even your parents' first marriages worked out, right? But what's <u>good</u> is that you're learning what to do when you get the 'big red F.' And you can't really succeed until you've learned that! Believe me?"

"Well . . ."

Joe stood up. "I think it's time for our last stop. I want you to see <u>yourself</u> 30 years from now!"

On to the last stop!

"Oh, oh," Jamie said, gulping, "that's going to be hard!"

Joe laughed. "Actually, you're absolutely right, Jamie. I myself find that it's **way** too hard for young people to see themselves when they're a lot older. I mean, nobody your age should have to worry about gray hair, right?"

This time Jamie laughed. "OK, Joe, so what's the plan from here?"

?????

"Well, it's like this, Jamie. You won't actually see yourself, but you <u>will</u> see where you work -- and how you're doing these days. The place is actually in this same city -- right across town, as a matter of fact."

"Sounds good," Jamie agreed, standing up. "Did I go into business like I said I wanted to?"

"Absolutely! Not only that, but it was a business not too much different from the one Chris started. And," Joe added, "your business actually had <u>more</u> problems in the first few years than the business Chris started. In fact, **you almost went <u>out</u>** of business a couple of times! But," Joe sighed, "I'm talking too much, as usual. Let's go see!"

Once again Joe raised both hands, snapped his fingers, and . . .

and . . . .

Jamie and Joe stood at a hallway window of another tall building, looking way down to the street below.

"Wow!" Jamie exclaimed while watching the people and the cars stream along.

"Great view, isn't it?" Joe asked.

"It sure is," Jamie responded. "What floor is this?"

"The 37th, but the view from your office is just as good." Joe started walking down the hallway, beckoning Jamie to follow.

Jamie and Joe stopped in front of a door with writing on it. Joe pointed to the door with his biggest smile yet. "CREATIVE DEVELOPMENT, INC.," the door read. "**JAMIE JOHNSON**, PRESIDENT AND CHIEF EXECUTIVE OFFICER."

CREATIVE DEVELOPMENT, INC.
JAMIE JOHNSON PRESIDENT AND CHIEF EXECUTIVE OFFICER

Jamie's eyes grew wider and wider as Jamie stared at the door. Jamie turned to Joe. "You mean . . . . . ."

"Listen," Joe said as the sound of voices came from behind the door.

"Jamie," said someone with an excited voice, "that's the <u>best</u> idea you've had in years. If we can complete this project the way you've outlined it, there's no telling how far we could go!"

Jamie wanted to listen more -- especially to one calm, convincing voice -- but Joe called Jamie to the other side of the hallway.

"Congratulations, dear Jamie," Joe said, shaking Jamie's hand, and Jamie could see a tear in Joe's eye. "But, Jamie, it's time for me to go."

Jamie was surprised. "Why, Joe? Do you have to?"

"I'm afraid so," Joe revealed. "Oh, one thing before you get back home, Jamie."

"What's that, Joe?"

???

???

"If you try to tell anybody about me, it won't work. I mean, you can try to talk about me, but the words won't come out right. You'll just be saying something else. You can tell Bosco about me, though. He's OK."

Jamie frowned in thought. "You mean, if I wanted to tell about you, I'd just start talking about the weather or something like that?"

Joe smiled his unforgettable smile. "Something like that."

"OK, Joe."

"If you say so."

There was a rather long silence. "Well, good-bye, Jamie," Joe concluded as he placed an arm on Jamie's shoulder. "Take this and remember me," Joe said, placing his baseball cap on Jamie's head. "And good luck in your next game, Jamie."

"Thanks, Joe," Jamie answered. "You're a real friend."

Jamie and Joe both smiled.

"Say," Jamie blurted, "didn't you say something about 'young people' a while back. I mean, do you do this kind of thing for lots of kids?

I thought you were in that bottle for the last 50 years. I mean..."

But Joe just winked, and...

Jamie was back in the attic.

Joe
was gone.

Jamie looked around, but even the strange-looking bottle wasn't there anymore.

Jamie picked up the baseball glove and trudged down the stairs to Jamie's room.

Sunny the hamster was squeaking away in the wheel inside his cage. On the bed sat Bosco, wagging his tail slowly and looking quite puzzled. Jamie sighed. "I <u>could</u> tell you all about it, old buddy," Jamie said, petting Bosco's head, but I don't think even <u>you'd</u> believe me!"

!

!!

Suddenly Jamie felt a little lonely. Jamie sat down at the desk and looked at the half-finished painting of Jamie's grandmother.

On one corner of the painting Jamie saw a small piece of paper Jamie hadn't noticed before. Jamie picked up the paper and read,

"OK, you found a better baseball glove, so how about finishing this painting?

"Your Friend,
Joe the 'Genie'"

P.S.:   You're a real
        winner, Jamie."

The next day the painting was done. Jamie proudly brought Mom and Dad to Jamie's room to see the finished picture.

"Jamie, it's lovely," Mom beamed as she hugged Jamie. "You did a great job!"

Jamie smiled. "Thanks, Mom. What do you think, Dad?"

Jamie's father ran his finger along his chin as he studied the completed portrait. "Well, Jamie, it's really very nice. You really did a terrific job. It really does look just like your grandmother. But . . . . ."

"But what, Dad?"

"Well, Jamie, I knew your grandmother very well, and . . . ."

"So?"

"Well, my memory may be slipping, but I think your grandmother's eyes were a little more blue. Not quite so gray. And when she was younger she was more of a blond. Her hair was a lot less brown than you show it here. Actually, I found some other pictures of her the other day which are clearer than that other one -- if you want to make your portrait better, that is."

There was a short silence as Dad handed Jamie the new photographs. Jamie slowly looked over the photographs.

Mom and Dad seemed to be waiting for Jamie's reaction. "It's OK. I can learn from this." Jamie paused. "And Dad," Jamie admitted, "you were absolutely right. I guess I could have been more careful. I see it now. Grandma's eyes and hair are not right at all."

Jamie looked at both parents. Neither one seemed to know quite what to say.

After a while Jamie's dad remarked, "You could just touch up those parts of your painting, Jamie, but I think it might mess up the whole thing."

"Right again, Dad," Jamie said, beaming. "Tell you what -- my birthday's in a few more weeks, right? How about an early present?"

"Maybe. What did you have in mind?"

Jamie smiled at both parents. "I'd like some more paints. And a new canvas. I want to paint this whole picture over -- and do it right!"

I want to paint this whole picture over -- and do it right!

Jamie's parents looked at each other. Then they both smiled.

"Of course," Jamie's mother replied. "If that's what you really want."

"Thanks, Mom and Dad!"

"By the way, Jamie," Mom added, "where did you get that new baseball cap? I don't recall ever seeing that one before."

??

???

????

"Oh, this one?" Jamie said as Jamie removed the cap and straightened out the brim. "Something I got from a very good friend." Jamie smiled once more and thought, "a really very good friend."

"I'll tell you about it sometime."

. . . . . **I'll tell you about it sometime. . .**

Jamie stood in left field, pounding the glove found weeks earlier in the attic. The wind blew into Jamie's face, sure to help any fly ball hit to the outfield. The crowd roared as the batter swung at the first pitch and fouled it off.

League Championship Game!

This was the League Championship game! One more out and they'd be in the playoffs!! Jamie's team was ahead by one run, but . . . the bases were loaded.

Another foul ball! Strike two!!

Jamie thought about what happened in the game so far. Jamie had done pretty well. Two hits and two runs batted in. True, Jamie had misplayed a line drive hit to left field in the first inning, but Jamie made up for it by throwing the runner out at third.

Chris had a triple and two home runs. But, Chris was almost thrown out of the game the last time up, when Chris argued with the umpire after being called out on strikes.

Outside. Ball one.

The wind continued to blow straight into Jamie's face. It even seemed to be getting stronger and stronger as the inning went on.

Just a little inside. Ball two.

Strangely, Jamie was thinking about Miss Mellon. On the last math test, a "C," Miss Mellon had written, "Much better, Jamie. You're making real progress. More learning and growth! Good for you!!"

!!!

More learning and growth!!

Jamie was wearing the team cap, of course, but in a back pocket could feel the special cap worn by Joe. Jamie wondered where Joe was now.

Outside again. Ball three. Oh, oh.

The crowd groaned. The pitcher walked off the mound and rubbed the ball really hard.

Behind the dugout Jamie could see Mom and Dad, standing up like everyone else, and cheering wildly. This was such a big game that even Jamie's brother Jimmy had come over to watch.

While looking at Mom and Dad Jamie remembered having just finished repainting the portrait of Jamie's grandmother that afternoon. It had turned out just right the second time, and Mom and Dad seemed really excited about it. Dad even suggested that Jamie try a couple of other portraits --

including Jamie's grand-father, and a cousin in Ohio.

The noise of the crowd grew and grew. People were yelling, and stomping on the bleachers. The next pitch would have to be over the plate, or the game would be tied!

The pitcher wound up, and threw a perfect strike right down the middle.

Jamie heard a sharp "crack" as the batter swung and launched a shot toward left field. Right toward Jamie.

Another line drive -- just like the one in the first inning!

But Jamie had learned from the earlier mistake. Line drives approached quickly, and you had to move fast.

Jamie sped back swiftly, then stopped a few feet short of the fence.

But . . .

The wind was stronger than Jamie thought! The ball was going to be over Jamie's head -- Jamie had stopped too soon!!

But . . .

It wasn't too late to jump.

It
wasn't
too
late . . . .
to
jump.

With all Jamie's strength Jamie leaped upward, and the ball snapped into the very top of the glove Jamie had found in the attic.

Jamie fell to the ground-- but hung on to the ball!

Jamie fell
to the ground
but
hung on to
the ball!

Jamie's team had won!

They were League Champions!!

League Champions!

As Jamie's teammates rushed out into the outfield, Jamie lay on the ground and laughed and smiled.

Because Jamie knew that this victory was something much bigger than a game. Something <u>much</u> more important.

Jamie knew that even if the ball had fallen to the ground, everything would still be OK. That Jamie would have other chances -- chances to learn and grow and do BETTER next time.

That <u>was</u>
THE
BIG
SECRET,
after all!

Jamie was no longer afraid of the "big red F!"

Jamie

was

no longer

afraid of the

"big red F!"

As happy as Jamie was when the whole team mobbed Jamie -- as good as Jamie felt at seeing the tears in Mom and Dad's eyes as they told Jamie, "Oh, Jamie, we couldn't be more proud!" -- Jamie felt even BETTER having learned the wonderful lesson Jamie's good friend Joe had taught Jamie.

Because now Jamie knew that, no matter what happened on the next test, or in the next game, or in whatever tomorrow might bring,

IT REALLY
IS OK
TO FAIL!! --

AS LONG
AS YOU LEARN
and GROW!!!!

Thanks,
Joe!

Jamie's Story

There's a story of Jamie I must tell.
In whatever Jamie did,
     Jamie did quite well.
But, out of the blue,
For no reason at all,
Jamie flunked a test
And dropped a fly ball.

Jamie wondered and wondered
What the problem must be,
And said over and over,
"There's something wrong with me!"

But Jamie found out
We all make mistakes.
Sometimes you must fail to win --
     and that's what it takes!

To learn, to grow,
To become ever stronger.
And this above all --
To fear failure no longer!

          -- Joe

MY IDEAS
about
the story!

1.   Describe a failure in your own life.

_____

_____

_____

_____

_____

How did it make you FEEL?

_____

_____

_____

_____

_____

2. What ACTION did you TAKE to make your failure BETTER?

_____

_____

_____

_____

_____

_____

If you TOOK NO ACTION, what ACTION could you have taken?

_____

_____

_____

_____

_____

3. In your own words, describe what you think Jamie learned about failure in this story.

_____

_____

_____

_____

_____

_____

_____

_____

_____

_____

_____

_____

4.   Obvously, Jamie will not win every game, do well on every test, or complete every project correctly.

What do you think Jamie's next "failure" might be?

_____

_____

_____

_____

How will Jamie handle this situation?

_____

_____

_____

_____

5. What do you think your next "failure" might be?

_____

_____

_____

_____

_____

How will you handle this situation?

_____

_____

_____

_____

_____

_____

_____

6. Do you think Jamie in this story is a BOY, or a GIRL?

_____

Why do you FEEL this way?

_____

_____

_____

_____

_____

_____

_____

_____

_____

_____

_____

_____

7.   Do you think Chris in this story is a BOY, or a GIRL?

_____

Why do you FEEL this way?

_____

_____

_____

_____

_____

_____

_____

_____

_____

_____

_____

_____

8. Do you know boys and girls who are like Chris?

_____

Do you still think these boys and girls are so lucky?

_____

Why?

_____

_____

_____

_____

_____

_____

_____

_____

_____

9. Do you FEEL BETTER about yourself now and the things that you can do?

_____

_____

Why?

_____

_____

_____

_____

_____

_____

_____

_____

_____

_____

Always remember you know. . . . "THE BIG SECRET"

**Show every child in
your life you . . . .
. . . . really care.
Share "The Big Secret."
We can help!**

- Better discounts available with higher
  quantities.
- Special discounts for schools and
  organizations.
- Learn other secrets of personal
  growth and motivation.
- See next pages for additional growth
  products.
- For additional copies call:

1-800-DR-JOHN-P
(1-800-375-6467)

Thank you for your order!
All personal growth materials are guaranteed. If you
are not satisfied simply return them for a full refund.

**Personal
Growth
Materials**

Available from
Pelizza & Associates

NEWSLETTER

"Pelizza's Positive Principles for Better Living"
    A bimonthly newsletter designed to help you feel **BETTER** and do **BETTER** by managing your THINKING and taking ACTION.

    Each issue includes an illustration of one of Dr. Pelizza's key principles for living more positively, stories from real life, letters and anecdotes from readers. There's even a recipe to help you eat **BETTER!**

    Each issue contains graphics that enhance the concepts and principles discussed.

    "Pelizza's Positive Principles for Better Living" is also the best way to keep up with Pelizza & Associates' newest publications, programs, and seminars.

ISSN 1070-6674 $12.00year, 6 issues @ 12 pages

AUDIO TAPES

"Keys to High Energy Living"

Dr. Pelizza illustrates several key principles which can increase the ENERGY you need to feel BETTER and do BETTER. He discusses the Principles of DISCOVERY, ACTION, GROWTH, and CLOSURE -- all of which, when applied in daily life, will enable you to live at a consistently higher level of ENERGY -- to feel BETTER and accomplish more every day.

$10.00, 60-minute audio tape

"Staying Motivated During Change"

Dr. Pelizza demonstrates what MOTIVATION is. How to create it in your life every day. How to MOTIVATE yourself and how to MOTIVATE others. You'll also learn to respond to CHANGE in ways that will ENERGIZE you instead of depress you.

Especially recommended for workers who need to respond POSITIVELY to changes in their professional life.

$10.00, 60-minute audio tape

"21 Ways to Get Up and Go!"

Dr. Pelizza illustrates 21 ways to create more energy in your life every day. The 21 ways are easy to incorporate into your lifestyle. You'll feel BETTER about yourself and do BETTER in your life every day.

Great way to keep yourself motivated on a daily basis and a tape you are sure to enjoy!

$10.00, 60-minute audio tape

BOOKS

"Foot in the Door"

Learn SELF-POWER CONCEPTS to lead a more POSITIVE and PRODUCTIVE life. SELF-POWER CONCEPTS refers to a body of knowledge about your own capacity to grow -- to be in control of your life, to think POSITIVELY and effectively, to set life goals, to manage stress, to benefit from failure, and to develop a personal affirmation program for yourself.

Features areas for listing your Life Goals and Action Plans. There is also a diary section for personal and professional growth.

ISBN 0-9614872-0-8   154 pages, paperback, $11.95

"Thoughts to Make you THINK . . . and FEEL BETTER"

Dr. Pelizza's collection of inspirational thoughts, and simple concepts about feeling BETTER and doing BETTER -- every day. You'll receive "food for thought" on a variety of topics, including change, choice, achievement, discipline, growth, and feeling BETTER!

Throughout the book there are twelve questions that help the reader identify what they really want in life.

This book makes an excellent gift and features a "to and from" page allowing you to write a personal thought to someone on a special occasion.

ISBN 0-9614872-1-6   87 pages , paperback, $11.95

"There's MAGIC in DISCOVERY!"

Dr. Pelizza tells you how to DISCOVER the ENERGY that can be yours every day of your life by harnessing the power of DISCOVERY. Begin by learning to recognize POSITIVE DISCOVERY in your life. Find out how to put yourself into DISCOVERY MODE and enjoy one POSITIVE DISCOVERY after another -- more and more ENERGY to feel BETTER and do BETTER!

Learn also how to use the PRINCIPLE OF ACTION to manage NEGATIVE DISCOVERY. Find out what to do when bad things happen, when life "hits" you in ways that reduce your ENERGY. DISCOVER how to bounce back more quickly and recover the ENERGY you need to feel BETTER -- GOOD -- TERRIFIC every day!

Features charts to help you monitor your progress in gaining more and more ENERGY from DISCOVERY.

ISBN 0-9614872-2-4   166 pages, paperback, $11.95

"The Big Secret"

Dr. Pelizza shares "The Big Secret". This book is designed for the elementary student but is appropriate for all ages. "The Big Secret" will give children an opportunity for real success!

Children will learn how to develop a stronger self-image, achieve better grades, become truly confident, discover their real talents and recover quickly from setbacks.

A simple POWERFUL concept which can CHANGE a child's life FOREVER!

ISBN 0-9614872-3-2   114 pages, paperback, $10.95

GUEST SPEAKER

Dr. Pelizza is available to speak to groups, schools, organizations, businesses and companies. He can tailor programs to meet your individual needs.

The following topics may be of interest to you:

- Self-esteem building for children

- There's MAGIC in DISCOVERY

- Stress Management for HIGH-ENERGY Living

- Staying Motivated during CHANGE

- Eight Habits for Mental Fitness

- The Common Link in Sales and Productivity

CONTACT: Pelizza & Associates
P.O. Box 225
North Chatham, N.Y. 12132
call
1-800-DR-JOHN-P
(1-800-375-6467)

or call

The Sage Colleges
Department of Health Education
Troy, New York 12180
(518) 270-2357

ABOUT THE AUTHOR

John J. Pelizza, Ph.D., is:

A leading authority on wellness, change process, motivation and stress management

A former department chairman of Health Education and former Wellness Director. Currently, John is a professor of Health Education, The Sage Colleges, Troy, New York

A dynamic speaker to over five hundred business, professional, and civic groups throughout the United States

The author of three other books:
Foot in the Door, a book on managing stress in your personal and professional life
Thoughts to Make You THINK and FEEL BETTER, a collection of inspirational quotes to make you think and feel better
There's Magic in Discovery, a book that illustrates many ways to enjoy the energy of positive discovery

The creator of "Pelizza's Positive Principles for Better Living," a newsletter about wellness, stress management, and personal growth

The creator and presenter of PPP, "Pelizza's Positive Principles", airing weekly on WPTR AM 1540, Schenectady, New York

The producer of three audio cassettes:
"Staying Motivated During Change", which deals with motivation and change in everyday life
"Keys to High Energy Living" which discusses the principles of Discovery, Action, Growth and Closure
"21 Ways to Get Up and Go!" which deals with practical ways to create energy

A winner of the "Outstanding Young Alumni Award" from Pittsburg State University, Pittsburg, Kansas

A former President of the New York State Public Health Association, Northeastern Region

The developer of a specialized Self-Power Concepts Program for Vietnam Veterans and their spouses

A contributor of articles to professional journals and health education text-books

The founder of Pelizza & Associates, an organization devoted to helping people attain personal growth and wellness -- to helping people feel BETTER and do BETTER

NOTES

NOTES

NOTES

NOTES